# THINGS TO MAKE AND DO

T0326177

# All About Eid

## SARAH SHAFFI
### ILLUSTRATED BY AALIYA JALEEL

**SCHOLASTIC**

Published in the UK by Scholastic Children's Books, 2021
Euston House, 24 Eversholt Street, London, NW1 1DB

A division of Scholastic Limited
London ~ New York ~ Toronto ~ Sydney ~ Auckland
Mexico City ~ New Delhi ~ Hong Kong

SCHOLASTIC and associated logos are trademarks and/or registered
trademarks of Scholastic Inc.

Text © Sarah Shaffi, 2021
Illustrations by Aaliya Jaleel

The right of Sarah Shaffi and Aaliya Jaleel to be identified as the author and
illustrator of this work respectively has been asserted by them in accordance with
the Copyright, Designs and Patents Act, 1988.

ISBN 978 0702 30292 3

A CIP catalogue record for this book is available from the British Library.

Printed and bound by Bell & Bain Ltd, UK

Papers used by Scholastic Children's Books are made from wood
grown in sustainable forests.

1 3 5 7 9 10 8 6 4 2

www.scholastic.co.uk

This copy of

# All About Eid: Things to Make and Do

belongs to:

_____

_____

Learn all about the Eid festivals celebrated by millions of
Muslims all over the world, every year, and the
events that lead up to them!

This book is packed full of crafts and delicious recipes
for you to make and share with friends and family.

Don't forget: you can find definitions of the words in **bold** in
the glossary at the back of the book.

# Islam Around the Globe

There are around 1.8 billion Muslims in the world, which is about a quarter of the world's population.

Most of the world's Muslims are one of two main **denominations**; around 87–90 per cent are Sunni Muslims, while around 10–13 per cent are Shia. However, even within these different denominations, there are many different groups of Muslims.

Different groups of Muslims practise their faith in different ways, but all Muslims believe in **Allah** (God) and celebrate both **Eid-ul-Fitr** and **Eid-ul-Adha**.

## DID YOU KNOW?

Indonesia has the largest population of Muslims – it is home to around 12 per cent of the world's Muslims.

Other countries that have a majority Muslim population include Pakistan, Saudi Arabia, Niger, Egypt, Somalia and the United Arab Emirates.

There are around 3 million Muslims living in the UK.

All
About
Eid

# What is Ramadan?

**Ramadan**, which leads up to Eid-ul-Fitr, is the ninth month of the Muslim lunar calendar. The month begins when a new moon is sighted. There's no way at the beginning of Ramadan to know exactly how many days the month is going to be, because it depends on when the next new moon is seen.

Muslims greet each other at the start of Ramadan by saying "Ramadan Mubarak", which means "have a blessed Ramadan". Each day during Ramadan, Muslims can't eat or drink anything from the moment the sun begins to rise to when it begins to set. This even includes water and chewing gum!

As well as not eating and drinking, people try to pray more and read the **Quran** during Ramadan. They try not to say bad words or argue and fight with people. Ramadan is about being kinder – to yourself and to everyone around you.

People wake up for breakfast, even if it's in the middle of the night. This meal is called **suhoor**. After eating, people do the early morning prayer, and then often go back to sleep. Muslims pray five times throughout the day; these prayers are called **Fajr**, **Duhur**, **Asr**, **Maghrib** and **Ishaa**.

In the evening, people open or "break" their fasts with a meal called **iftar**. It is traditional to eat a date and then drink some water to open the fast, before having a proper meal. During Ramadan, people hold evening feasts, where they invite family and friends over to break the fast with them.

As well as being a religious month where Muslims seek to gain a better relationship with Allah, Ramadan is also about community and making time for loved ones.

Ishaa (the last prayer of the day for Muslims) is prayed a little differently during the month of Ramadan. It includes **taraweeh**, which is a long but very special prayer, just for the month of Ramadan. In a mosque, the **imam** leads these prayers. During the course of the month, the imam will recite the whole of the Quran, in small sections in the correct order.

In the last ten days of Ramadan, there is a special night called **Laylat-al-Qadr**, meaning Night of Power. It is not known exactly when this is, but it falls on one of the odd numbered nights, and many people mark it on the 27th night of Ramadan. This marks the night when the Quran was first revealed to the **Prophet** Muhammad (**pbuh**).

In some countries, fasts can be very long because the days are much longer. Ramadan ends when the new moon is sighted, and the next day is Eid-ul-Fitr.

## WHAT IS A LUNAR CALENDAR?

A **lunar calendar** uses the moon instead of the sun to mark out months. In the Muslim calendar, a new lunar month begins when you can see a thin crescent of a new moon in the night sky.

## DID YOU KNOW?

Some people don't have to fast during Ramadan. This includes elderly people, children, ill people and pregnant women. That's because it wouldn't be healthy for these people to go too long without food and drink.

# My Ramadan Tracker

Use this chart to track the month of Ramadan by colouring in a star at the end of each day.

| | | | | |
|---|---|---|---|---|
| 1 | 2 | 3 | 4 | 5 |
| 6 | 7 | 8 | 9 | 10 |
| 11 | 12 | 13 | 14 | 15 |
| 16 | 17 | 18 | 19 | 20 |
| 21 | 22 | 23 | 24 | 25 |
| 26 | 27 | 28 | 29 | 30 |

## TOP TIP:

Use a different colour for days when you tried to fast – even if it was just for an hour or two!

# Eid-ul-Fitr

Eid-ul-Fitr translates to **FESTIVAL OF THE BREAKING OF THE FAST** and takes place on the first day of the 10th month of the Islamic calendar, the day after the last fasting day of Ramadan.

Celebrations start with morning prayers, and then it's all about eating delicious food, giving presents and spending time with family and friends.

Eid-ul-Fitr is a public holiday in Islamic countries. In fact, some countries like Dubai and Pakistan even make it a three-day mandated holiday.

**Saum** means fasting and is one of the **Five Pillars of Islam**, along with **shahada**, **zakaat**, **salaah** and **Hajj**.

## WHO DECIDES WHEN IT'S EID-UL-FITR?

Eid-ul-Fitr depends on the sighting of a new moon, but whose job is it to look for that moon? In Muslim countries, there is usually a group or committee of people who look for the moon!

In non-Muslim countries, local or regional mosques will look for the moon and announce when they have seen it. It is also common for citizens of non-Muslim countries to follow Saudi Arabia and await their announcement.

# Eid-ul-Adha

Hajj is a pilgrimage that takes places in the 12th month of the Islamic calendar. The celebration after Hajj is Eid-ul-Adha, which translates to the **FESTIVAL OF THE SACRIFICE.**

This Eid focuses on the remembrance of Prophet Ibrahim's (pbuh) sacrifice and as well as the usual celebrations and festivities, focuses even more on feeding the less fortunate.

# All About Hajj

All Muslims, if they are well enough, debt free and can afford it, are required to go on Hajj once in their lifetime. Millions of people from around the world go to observe Hajj in Saudi Arabia each year.

Everyone, whatever their background, is equal on Hajj. This is signified by their clothing: for Hajj, everyone wears white – an outfit called **ihram**. There are a number of different steps to Hajj:

### DAY ONE

**Pilgrims** will put on their ihram and walk seven times around the **Kabah** in **Mecca**'s Masjid-al-Haram, also known as the Grand Mosque. They then travel to **Mina**, where they spend the night in a campsite.

### DAY TWO

The pilgrims then travel to the plains of Arafat, outside Mecca, where they spend the day praying. In the evening, the pilgrims travel to Muzdalifah, where they collect stones for the next day.

### DAY THREE

Pilgrims go back to Mina, where they head to three pillars called Jamarat, and they throw stones at the largest of these pillars. It is now Eid-ul-Adha, which will be celebrated by Muslims around the world while the pilgrims continue on their journey.

Many pilgrims go back to Mecca where they will again circle the Kabah seven times, and then walk between the small hills of **Safa and Marwa** – which are in the Grand Mosque – seven times. They then return to the campsite at Mina.

## WHAT ARE SAFA AND MARWA?

Safa and Marwa are two small hills in Mecca, now located in the Grand Mosque. It is symbolic for Muslims as they believe this is where the Prophet Ibrahim's (pbuh) wife, Hajar, went in search of water. She travelled seven times between the hills of Safa and Marwa before the angel Gabriel came to her aid, revealing a spring of water.

That position is now known as the zamzam well, and pilgrims to Mecca drink this holy water on their visit.

## DAY FOUR AND FIVE

On each day, the pilgrims will throw seven stones at each of the three pillars in Mina. They'll spend a couple more days in Mina, before returning once more to Mecca to circle the Kabah for a final seven times.

Many pilgrims then choose to go to the city of **Medina** in Saudi Arabia, where the Prophet Muhammad (pbuh) is buried. This is not, however, a required part of Hajj.

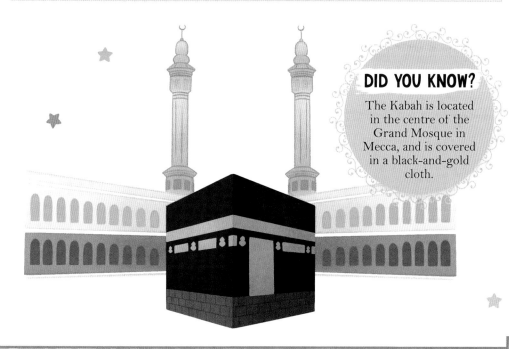

### DID YOU KNOW?

The Kabah is located in the centre of the Grand Mosque in Mecca, and is covered in a black-and-gold cloth.

# Eid Prayers

Special prayers take place to mark both Eid-ul-Fitr and Eid-ul-Adha. Most people go to **mosques** to perform salaah. There are many different types of mosques - some are large, some are small. Some have domes and minarets, while others have intricate mosaics. Here are some of the beautiful mosques around the world where people go for Eid prayers.

## MASJID AL-HARAM, MECCA, SAUDI ARABIA

The Masjid al-Haram, also known as the Grand Mosque, is the holiest site in Islam. The large mosque is where you go to begin the Hajj pilgrimage, and where you also go to do the smaller Umrah pilgrimage. The mosque can hold 1.5 million people at one time. At its centre is the Kabah.

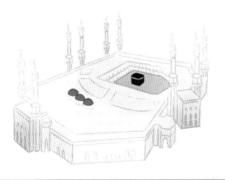

## SHEIKH ZAYED GRAND MOSQUE, ABU DHABI, UNITED ARAB EMIRATES

This mosque was finished in 2007 and has the world's biggest hand-knotted carpet, which was created by more than 12,000 artisans, and there is a 12-tonne crystal chandelier in the mosque. This mosque can hold 40,000 worshippers, and it's popular with visitors who come to see its stunning design, including its 82 domes and its reflecting pools.

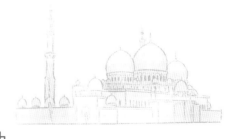

## MASJID AN-NABAWI, MEDINA, SAUDI ARABIA

This is the second holiest mosque in Islam, and it is the resting place of the Prophet Muhammad (pbuh). It can hold around 1 million people for prayers.

## THE FAISAL MOSQUE OF ISLAMABAD, PAKISTAN

Construction of this mosque began in 1976 and its size makes it the fourth largest mosque in the world! It has a unique geometric design and is said to hold about 300,000 worshippers.

## LONDON CENTRAL MOSQUE, LONDON, ENGLAND

This mosque is also known to many as Regent's Park Mosque because of its location near the famous Regent's Park in London. The mosque was finished in 1977, and the main hall of the mosque can hold 5,000 worshippers.

## THE SULTAN AHMED MOSQUE (ALSO KNOWN AS THE BLUE MOSQUE), ISTANBUL, TURKEY

This mosque, found in Turkey's capital Istanbul, is also known as the Blue Mosque because of its blue tiles. It was built between 1609 and 1616 during the rule of Ahmed I. Around 10,000 people can pray in the mosque at any one time.

# Eid Outfits

Both Eid-ul-Fitr and Eid-ul-Adha are a time for people to dress up. Here's a quick look at traditional Eid outfits in just a handful of different countries and cultures around the world.

## PAKISTAN

In Pakistan many people will wear shalwar kameez (a long top over a pair of trousers). Men might put a decorative waistcoat on top, and have a topi – a hat that they wear for prayers. Women's shalwar kameez will often be in bright colours, and can have lace, ribbon and sequins.

Women will usually wear a matching head covering, as well, often called a dupatta.

## SOMALIA

Women in Somalia will often wear a beautiful abaya (a long dress, often black, worn by Muslim women) or a **dirac** (a type of long dress that is traditional to Somalia and is often worn on celebratory occasions such as weddings and festivities). Men may wear a **khamiis** with patterns or a plain khamiis with a shawl thrown over one shoulder.

## NIGERIA

Women in Nigeria will often wear an abaya. The fabric might be printed with beautiful and colourful patterns, and they will often have a matching headscarf or head covering made out of the same patterned material.

Men might wear a kaftan, and this could be long (all the way down to their ankles) or short (to their thighs).

## INDONESIA

Men in Indonesia might wear the traditional baju koko, which is a collarless shirt with traditional embroidered designs. It will be worn with a sarung, which is a type of kilt or sarong, made from a woven cloth.

While women wear traditional dress called **kebaya kurung**, which is made up of a blouse (kebaya) and a long skirt, or a blouse dress. Items are traditionally made from batik – an ancient form of dyeing a fabric in many different colours and patterns – or involve lace fabrics.

# The Gift of Giving

Eid is a time for celebrating, but it's also a time for charitable giving and kindness.

Before and during Ramadan, many Muslims give money to those in need. This is called zakat and is given by all Muslims, regardless of what denomination or **sect** they are from.

However, there is also a form of charitable giving called **fitrana** that is specific to Eid-ul-Fitr. Fitrana is either (roughly) £5 or a charitable food donation. It should be paid by every adult Muslim who has food in excess of their needs, and it needs to be paid before the Eid prayer is performed during Eid-ul-Fitr.

Zakat and fitrana both go to those classified as poor or in need, and includes those who don't have enough money to feed themselves.

## DID YOU KNOW?

Zakat is obligatory, which means it is something each adult Muslim is required to do.

# Eid Mubarak Calligraphy

The traditional greeting on both Eid-ul-Fitr and Eid-ul-Adha is "**Eid Mubarak**" which means "Blessed Festival". This is Arabic, and many people say this to each other even if they don't speak Arabic.

Use the next page to practice writing Eid Mubarak in **calligraphy** some more!

# Make an Eid Card

## You will need:

- A4 coloured card
- A pen or pencil
- Glitter
- Glue
- Star stickers

## Instructions:

**1.** First, take your A4 coloured card and fold it in half so that it opens up like a book.

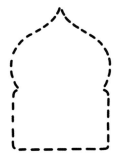

**2.** Once you have folded the sheet, draw a simple outline of a mosque (as shown here). Make sure it's nice and big.

**3.** Then, carefully cut out part of the outline as shown in the illustration for this step. Make sure you don't cut ALL the way round, leave the folded side as is!

**4.** Now you have a card in the shape of a mosque!

**5.** Decorate the front as you wish using your colouring pencils, glitter and star stickers. Then, write your Eid message on the inside!

**6.** Your card is now ready to gift!

HAPPY EID

## TOP TIP:
Try making a card using different shapes, such as a star or crescent!

# Make an Eid Bookmark

## You will need:

- An A4 sheet of thin card, in your choice of colour
- A 30cm ruler
- A pencil
- Scissors
- A holepunch
- Colouring pens or pencils
- A thin ribbon

## Instructions:

1. Take your card, and set your ruler along a short edge of the paper. Draw a line along the edge of the ruler 3–4cm from the edge of the paper.

2. Cut along the line you have drawn. This is your bookmark.

3. Punch a hole at one short end of the bookmark you've just cut.

4. Using a coloured pen, write "Eid Mubarak" on both sides of the bookmark. (You can even write it in Arabic on one side, using what you learned from pages 20–21, and then flip it over and write in English on the other side.)

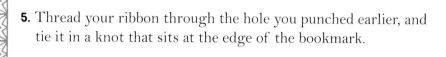

5. Thread your ribbon through the hole you punched earlier, and tie it in a knot that sits at the edge of the bookmark.

6. Trim your ribbon so it's about 2.5cm long on both sides. Your bookmark is now ready to put in your favourite book!

## TOP TIP:

If you have access to a laminator, laminate your bookmark to make it last a lot longer! If you decide to laminate your bookmark, punch the hole for the ribbon after you've laminated it, and not before.

# Make Eid Bunting

## You will need:

- Five sheets of A4 coloured card
- A pencil
- A ruler
- Scissors
- String or ribbon
- A holepunch
- Colouring pens and pencils, or paint
- Glue (optional)

## Instructions:

1. Using a ruler, draw a triangle the size of half of the page on a piece of A4 card and then cut it out. Repeat on the other half of the page and cut that out too.

2. Tracing around your first triangle piece, draw this out on four more pieces of coloured A4. You should be able to make two triangles for each A4 sheet.

**3.** Cut all the triangles out and lay them out in the order you want them to go on the bunting. Now write out "Eid Mubarak" on the bunting, putting one letter on each triangle until you have the entire phrase spelled out.

**4.** Using the hole punch make two holes on each triangle – one in each corner of the shortest edge.

**5.** Take your string and put it in the first hole of the first triangle, going from the back to the front. Pull it along the front of the triangle, then put it through the second hole, so it's now at the back again.

**6.** Now thread it through the first hole of the next triangle, and then repeat the above.

**7.** Do this until all the triangles are hanging from the string. Make sure to leave a small gap between the two words – 'Eid' and 'Mubarak'.

**8.** Space the triangles out evenly. You can, if you like, use a tiny bit of glue to stick the triangles into place. This will also help stop the small gap from closing.

## TOP TIP:

Use several different colours of card to get an even more colourful effect!

# Colour Your Own Mosque

You've already learnt about some of the most famous and beautiful mosques in the world, and now you can colour in your own on these pages. This mosque is pictured against the night sky, with plenty of stars and a crescent moon. Many big mosques are lit up at night, so you'll be able to see all sorts of colours.

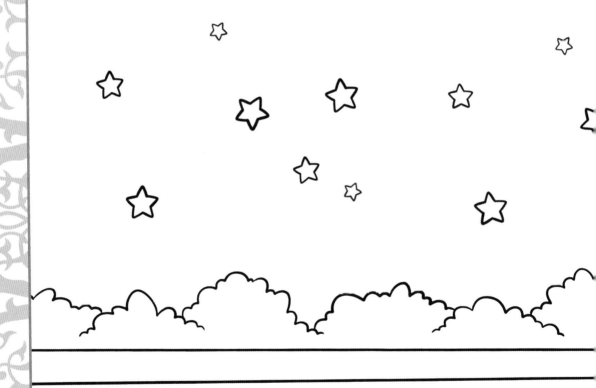

# Make a Decorative Placeholder

If you have friends and family coming for a delicious meal on Eid (or during Ramadan), why not make placeholders to show everyone where they need to sit? The placeholder can also be something people take with them after the meal as a reminder of the special occasion.

## Makes 4 placeholders

## You will need:

- A sheet of A4 card
- Scissors
- A pen
- Colouring pens or pencils
- Glitter pens

## Instructions:

1. Fold your A4 card in half lengthways, then open up and fold in half the other way.

2. Cut along the lines you've folded so you have four smaller cards.

3. Take one of the cards and fold in half along the short edge.

**4.** With your pen, write the name of your guest on one side of the card.

**5.** Now use your colouring pencils to decorate both sides of the card. You can decorate the placeholders with patterns or even glitter to add an extra sparkle.

**6.** Repeat steps 4 and 5 for all the placeholders.

**7.** When you're ready to use them, just unfold them slightly so they can stand up on their own and place them at the right place on the table.

## TOP TIP:

On the other side of the card (the side that doesn't have their name) you can write "Eid Mubarak" or a little Eid message to make your guest smile!

# Decorate Your Own Candle

Let your imagination run wild with this candle, which makes a beautiful gift.

## You will need:

- A cream pillar candle
- Masking tape
- Candle paint in purple (you can find these in craft shops or ask an adult to buy them for you online)
- Paintbrush
- Candle paint in gold
- PVA glue
- Glitter

## Instructions:

1. Cut two lengths of masking tape, long enough to go round the candle. Stick one about 2.5cm from the bottom of the candle and one 2.5cm from the top of the candle. You should now have a window in the middle.

2. Squeeze some of the purple candle paint on to a plate (use an old one that you don't need for food) or into an old, washed yoghurt pot. Using a paintbrush, paint the area between the masking tape.

**3.** Wait for it to dry completely – this will take a few hours.

**4.** With the gold candle paint, write "Eid Mubarak" on the area you've painted purple.

**5.** Once it's all dry, you can take the masking tape off.

**6.** Now it's time to decorate using your glitter and sequins.

**7.** Your candle is now ready to gift.

## TOP TIP:

You can use a coloured candle if you wish, just make sure you use candle paint that will show up against it.

### SAFETY FIRST

Remember to ask an adult for help if and when lighting a candle.

# Draw Your Own Henna Patterns

**Henna** is a natural reddish-brown dye that people use to decorate their hands and feet, and also sometimes to dye their hair. In Urdu and Hindi, it is called mehndi.

You can make many intricate patterns using henna, and the design will last for around a week on skin.

Henna goes on wet, and you have to leave it to dry completely before scraping it off. The longer you leave it, the darker the pattern will be. If you've got wet henna on your hands and feet, be careful not to touch anything, as you'll leave behind reddish-brown marks!

## TOP TIP:

Here is an example of a henna design. Colour it in and then use it as inspiration to create your own design on the blank hand opposite.

# Make a Moon and Stars Mobile

A mobile will bring a pop of magic and sparkle to a room, and if you hang it somewhere with a light breeze, it will flutter gently as well.

## You will need:

- A4 sheet of white card
- A sheet of tracing paper
- A pen or pencil
- Gold and silver paint
- String
- Holepunch
- Scissors

## Instructions:

1. Carefully trace the moon and the star on the next page on to your tracing paper and then cut them out.

2. Using the moon stencil you've created, draw an outline of a moon on your piece of card and cut it out.

3. Then using the star stencil, draw six stars on the card and cut those out separately so you have six stars.

**4.** Paint one side of the moon with the gold paint, and one side of all the stars with the silver paint.

**5.** When dry, turn all the stars and moon over and paint the other sides too.

**6.** Take your string and cut it into seven pieces, all different lengths.

**7.** When your moon and stars are completely dry, use the hole punch to punch one hole at the top of each star. Punch six holes along the outside bottom edge of the moon.

## SAFETY FIRST

Remember to be careful with scissors and ask an adult for help as they can be very sharp.

**8.** Thread six of your pieces of string through the holes in the moon and tie in a double knot at the back.

**9.** Take a star and thread one of the pieces of string through the star and tie in a double knot.

**10.** Do this for all the stars, until they're all hanging from the moon. If some of the knots have extra string, trim them, but make sure your knot is really tight and you don't cut the string off too close to it.

**11.** Punch a hole at the top of the moon and thread the seventh and final piece of string through it, securing it with a double knot.

**12.** Now choose a place to hang your mobile, and either tie it or stick it in place, so the stars hang down.

## TOP TIP:

Use a piece from a cardboard box to make the moon instead of standard card! It's sturdier and recycling is always a positive.

# Make an Eid Magnet

This lovely magnet will take pride of place on your fridge!

## You will need:

- Air-drying clay (you can find these in craft shops or ask an adult to buy them for you online)
- Poster paint in dark blue and gold
- Paintbrushes
- One self-adhesive magnetic disc (you can find these in craft shops or ask an adult to buy them for you online)

## Instructions:

1. Following the instructions on the air-drying clay, make a circle about the size of a glass. You might not need all the clay.

2. Wait for the clay to completely dry.

3. Paint one side of the clay circle with the dark blue paint.

4. Once the paint has dried completely, paint a gold moon in the centre.

5. When the gold paint is dry, turn the clay circle over and stick the self-adhesive magnetic disc in the centre.

6. Find the perfect spot on the fridge to put your magnet and stick it on!

# Make a Lantern

This lantern is super simple to make, and will light up a room beautifully.

## You will need:

- 2 sheets of coloured A4 paper
- A 30cm ruler
- A pencil
- Scissors
- Star stickers
- Glue
- A stapler
- A battery-powered tea light candle

**SAFETY FIRST**

Be careful with scissors and ask an adult for help when using a stapler.

## Instructions:

**1.** Take one sheet of the A4 card and fold it in half lengthways.

**2.** You now need to cut horizontal lines, each about 5cm long, from the folded edge. You need eight cuts in total, and they should be an equal distance apart. But make sure you don't cut all the way through.

**3.** Unfold the paper and put glue along one of the short edges.

**4.** Bring the short edges together and seal, keeping any sides with pencil markings on the inside, so you can't see it.

**5.** Press down lightly to make the cuts you've made open up.

**6.** Now take the other A4 sheet of card and cut a 1cm strip from the short side.

**7.** Staple one end of the small strip to one side of the lantern, and then curve it and staple the other end to the opposite side. This is your handle. Then, use your star stickers to decorate!

**8.** Switch on a battery-powered tea light candle, place the lantern over it and watch as your very own lantern lights up the room!

## TOP TIPS:

You can keep your lantern plain, or you can decorate it. If you want to decorate it, do so before cutting the slits into it. You can decorate the entire sheet, or you could draw a pattern along the two long edges to form a border.

You can also make the handle a different colour to the rest of the lantern for an extra pop of colour.

# Make an Eid Gift Box

If you want to give someone a unique Eid present, why not create a gift box just for them? Decorate a box using the tips below, and fill it with all the brilliant and beautiful creations you have made using this book so far.

## You will need:

- A shoebox with a lid
- Patterned wrapping paper
- Sticky tape
- A pencil
- Coloured card
- A glue stick
- Star stickers
- Colouring pens or pencils
- 4 sheets of coloured tissue paper

## Instructions:

**1.** Cover the lid and the box in wrapping paper, using the tape to secure it neatly on the inside.

**2.** Draw the letters E, I, D, M, U, B, A, R, A and K out on your coloured card, then carefully cut them out – make sure to ask an adult to help you with the scissors.

**3.** Stick the letters on the lid of the shoebox, with "Eid" on one line and "Mubarak" underneath.

**4.** Use your colouring pens or pencils, and your star stickers to decorate the box.

**5.** Scrunch up three of your tissue papers sheets lightly, and place inside the box.

**6.** Put the fourth sheet of tissue paper over the scrunched-up sheets, tucking it in at the sides to create a cushion for the gifts.

**7.** Fill your box with gifts, and your present is ready. Whoever receives this gift box will feel really special!

**TOP TIP:**
You could also use this decorated box for your own keepsakes - use it to save Eid cards and other gifts that you've been given.

# Recipes

## SAFETY FIRST

Remember to ask an adult for help when
using any sharp equipment, such as knives,
or attempting a recipe that requires the use
of an oven or hob.

And have fun creating and sharing
these delicious treats!

# Samosas *(stuffed pastries)*

Many cultures around the world make some sort of stuffed pastry, and they're all delicious! Samosas can be found in lots of countries around the world, from Nigeria to Somalia to India to Pakistan. These samosas are stuffed with potatoes and peas, but you can replace the peas with beans, sweetcorn or veg of your choice, as long as they're cut up small enough to cook thoroughly. Samosas are usually fried, but this version is baked.

## Makes 12

## Ingredients

- 2 medium potatoes, peeled
- 1 small onion
- 1 garlic clove
- 1 tbsp vegetable oil, plus a bit extra
- ½ tsp chilli powder
- 1 tsp ground coriander
- ½ tsp salt
- 2 tbsp peas
- 75g butter
- 12 sheets filo pastry
- Plain yoghurt or chutney, to serve

## Equipment

- Saucepan
- Frying pan
- Baking tray
- Greaseproof paper

## SAFETY FIRST

Ask an adult for help when using a knife or an oven.

# Method

**1.** Cut the potatoes into small, even-sized pieces and place in a pan of boiling water. Boil until soft, drain and then mash.

**2.** Chop the onion finely and crush the garlic clove.

**3.** Heat the oil in a frying pan and, when hot, add the onion. Fry gently until golden, then add the garlic and fry for another minute.

**4.** Add the chilli powder, ground coriander and salt, then mix for 30 seconds.

**5.** Add the peas and cook for 2–3 minutes before adding the mashed potatoes, stir, and cook for a few minutes more. Remove from the heat and let the mixture cool.

**6.** Meanwhile, melt the butter in a small pan or bowl. Turn the oven on to 200°C/400°F/Gas 6.

**7.** To assemble, take a sheet of filo pastry and put it on the worktop with the long edge facing you. Brush the middle of the pastry with butter and fold the top third over it. Now, brush the folded part with butter and fold the bottom third over it. You should now have a long strip of pastry.

**8.** Take a spoonful of the potato and pea mixture and put it at one end of the strip of pastry, a few centimetres from the edge.

**9.** Fold the short edge diagonally over the filling, making the start of a triangle. Keep folding along the strip until you reach the end of the pastry and have a triangle-shaped parcel. Seal the last fold with some of the melted butter.

**10.** Repeat steps 8–9 until you've used all the filo pastry sheets and the filling mixture – it makes 12. If you have any mixture left over, you can eat it as is!

**11.** Line a baking tray with greaseproof paper and brush with a little oil.

**12.** Arrange the samosas on the tray. Bake for 15 minutes, then turn over and cook for another 15–20 minutes, until golden brown. If you like, serve them with yoghurt or chutney.

# Bolani *(stuffed flatbread)*

Bolani is a stuffed flatbread from Afghanistan traditionally filled with potatoes, spring onions and coriander, but other fillings can include lentils, pumpkin and leeks. You can serve it with plain yoghurt, but it's also great with sweet chilli sauce, and even ketchup!

## Makes 8

## Ingredients

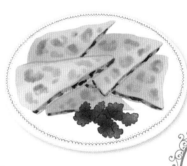

### For the dough

- 300g plain flour
- 1 tbsp olive oil, plus extra for cooking bolani
- 1 tsp salt
- About 250ml warm water

### Equipment

- 2 mixing bowls
- Baking tray
- 2 saucepans
- Rolling pin
- Frying pan

### For the filling

- 3 medium Maris Piper potatoes, peeled
- 1 tsp butter
- 200g baby spinach leaves
- 50g spring onions
- 2 tbsp chopped fresh coriander
- 1 tsp chilli flakes
- Salt, to taste

# Method

1. First, make the dough by mixing together the flour, olive oil and salt in a mixing bowl, then stir in 100ml of the warm water with a spoon. Add another 100ml of the water and this time use your hands to mix.

2. Knead the dough until it is smooth and springy. If it is too dry, add a tiny bit more water, 1 tablespoon at a time so that the dough doesn't become too wet, and mix it in well.

3. Split the dough into eight equal-sized pieces and roll each piece into a ball. Put on a baking tray, cover with cling film and set to one side.

4. Next, make the filling. Cut the potatoes into small cubes and place in a pan of boiling water. Boil until soft, then drain and mash with the butter.

5. Meanwhile, wash the spinach. Put it in a pan and cook for 2 minutes until the leaves wilt. Put the spinach in a colander and when cool, squeeze the leaves with your hands to remove as much water as possible, then roughly chop.

6. Chop the spring onions and put them in a bowl with the mashed potato, spinach, coriander and chilli flakes and mix together. Add salt, to taste, and mix again.

7. Take a ball of dough and roll out to a circle a bit bigger than a side plate (around 20cm). You may need to dust your work surface and rolling pin with plain flour to stop the dough sticking!

8. Spread 1 tablespoon of the potato and spinach mixture on to half of the dough circle, then bring the other half over to make a thin half-moon-shaped parcel. Use a fork to press the edges together to seal. Repeat this with the remaining dough balls.

9. To cook, heat a little olive oil in a frying pan and, when hot, carefully add a bolani. Cook for 3–4 minutes, then drizzle a little more oil over the uncooked side and carefully turn the bolani over. Cook for another 3–4 minutes before removing to a plate. The bolani should be golden brown on both sides.

10. Repeat to cook eight bolani in total, then serve hot.

# Cholay *(chickpea curry)*

You might think that chickpea curry is a dinner dish, but it's actually a popular breakfast dish in some countries, especially on Eid. Many people in countries like Pakistan and India will go home from Eid prayers and eat chickpea curry with parathas, followed by halwa.

## Serves 4

### Ingredients

- 1 white onion
- 1 tbsp vegetable oil
- 1 garlic clove
- 1cm piece of root ginger
- ¾ tsp salt
- 1 tsp chilli powder
- ½ tsp turmeric powder
- 1 tsp ground coriander
- ½ tsp garam masala
- ½ tin chopped tomatoes
- 400g tin chickpeas
- 2 tbsp plain yoghurt
- Parathas, to serve

### Equipment

- Deep, heavy-bottomed saucepan

# Method

**1**. Halve the onion and cut into thin slices.

**2**. Heat oil in a deep, heavy-bottomed saucepan and when hot, add the onion slices. Cook gently over a medium heat until the onion is soft.

**3**. Crush the garlic clove and finely chop the ginger. Add both to the pan and cook for 1 minute.

**4**. Turn the heat down to low and pour in a small amount of water, just enough to cover the bottom of the pan.

**5**. Add the salt and all the dry spices – chilli powder, turmeric, ground coriander and garam masala – and stir thoroughly.

**6**. Mix in the chopped tomatoes. Simmer slowly over a low heat until the oil separates from the tomatoes when you run a wooden spoon through the curry.

**7**. Drain the chickpeas and add to the curry, and stir thoroughly.

**8**. Pop the lid on the pan and simmer gently for around 15–20 minutes, checking every 5 minutes and stirring until thickened.

**9**. Stir in the yoghurt. Cook for 1 minute, then switch off the heat and serve with parathas.

**SAFETY FIRST**
Ask an adult for help when using a knife or a hob.

# Namak Para *(pastry snacks)*

These delicious savoury snacks are very simple to make. Be warned though, you'll want to eat them all in one go!

## Makes lots!

## Ingredients

- 125g plain flour, plus extra for dusting
- ½ tsp cumin seeds
- ½ tsp salt
- 50ml water
- Oil, for frying

**SAFETY FIRST**
Ask an adult for help when using a knife or a hob.

## Equipment

- Mixing bowl
- Rolling pin
- Deep, heavy-bottomed saucepan

## Method

**1.** Put the plain flour, cumin seeds and salt in a mixing bowl and stir.

**2.** Add 50ml water and mix with a spoon until the dough begins to come together. If the dough is too dry, add a little bit more water, 1 tablespoon at a time so it doesn't become too wet, and mix it in well.

**3.** Using your hands, knead the dough until smooth and springy.

**4.** Sprinkle a little flour on the worktop. Cut the dough in half and roll it out until the same thickness as a 50p coin.

**5.** Using a sharp knife, make diagonal cuts into the dough, about 1cm apart. Make diagonal cuts in the opposite direction to form diamond-shaped pieces of dough.

**6.** Repeat steps 4 and 5 with the remaining half of dough.

**7.** Get an adult to help with the next bit. Heat enough oil to deep-fry the dough pieces in a deep, heavy-bottomed saucepan.

**8.** When the oil is hot, carefully drop some of the diamond pieces of dough into the hot oil and deep fry until golden brown and crisp. You will need to do this in batches so they don't stick together.

**9.** Drain the namak para on kitchen paper and leave them to cool. They're now ready to eat!

# Tabbouleh *(parsley salad)*

This delicious salad involves a lot of chopping by hand - ask a grown up to help, if you like! You could also use a food processor, but be careful not to chop the vegetables too finely or they'll become mushy. Serve the salad on the side of any savoury dish.

## Serves 6

## Ingredients

- 50g bulgur wheat
- 100g flat-leaf parsley
- 50g fresh mint
- 2 tomatoes
- 3 spring onions
- 3 tbsp olive oil
- 2 lemons
- Salt and pepper

## Equipment

- Saucepan
- Serving bowl

# Method

**1.** Cook the bulgur wheat according to the packet instructions, then drain through a sieve and leave to cool.

**2.** Carefully, chop the parsley as finely as possible. Put it in a serving bowl that's big enough for all the salad ingredients, and also to mix everything together without it falling out!

**3.** Now chop the mint finely and add to the bowl.

**4.** Cut the tomatoes in half and scoop out the seeds with a teaspoon. Discard the seeds, finely chop the tomatoes and add to the bowl.

**5.** Finally, chop the spring onions into tiny pieces and add to the bowl.

**6.** Mix everything together, then add the bulgur wheat and olive oil. Squeeze the juice from the lemons into the bowl.

**7.** Check the flavour, then add salt and pepper to taste. Mix again, and the tabbouleh is ready to serve.

**SAFETY FIRST**
Ask an adult for help when using a knife or a hob.

# Chaat *(chickpea salad)*

Chaat is a delicious cold salad from countries including Pakistan, India and Bangladesh. It's often served there as a street food, because it's so simple and tasty. You can add a chopped chilli to the top, but if you don't like spicy food, then leave it off.

## Serves 4

## Ingredients

- 2 400g tins chickpeas
- 2 medium potatoes, peeled
- 1 tsp garam masala
- 1 red onion
- 1 tomato
- 4 tbsp plain yoghurt
- 3 tsp chaat masala
- 2 tbsp tamarind sauce, plus more to serve
- 1 handful of fresh coriander
- 1 red chilli (optional)

## Equipment

- Saucepan
- Serving bowl

**SAFETY FIRST**
Ask an adult for help when using a knife or a hob.

# Method

**1**. Drain the chickpeas and put into a large serving bowl.

**2**. Cut the potatoes into small cubes and place in a pan of boiling water with the garam masala. Boil until soft, then drain and set aside to cool.

**3**. Chop the red onion and the tomato into small pieces.

**4**. Add the onion, tomato and potatoes to the bowl of chickpeas and mix together until combined.

**5**. Now, add the rest of the ingredients. Dot spoonfuls of the yoghurt over the top of the chickpea salad.

**6**. Sprinkle with the chaat masala and then dot the tamarind on top.

**7**. Chop the coriander and the chilli (if using) and sprinkle these over the top.

**8**. The chaat is now ready to serve – ask everyone to help themselves, adding more toppings if they wish (see Top Tip, below).

## TOP TIP:

Everyone has different tastes, so give them the option of adapting their chaat. Have extra of the following in small bowls when you serve:

- Chopped red onion
- Tamarind sauce
- Chaat masala
- Chopped chilli
- Chopped coriander

# Pakoras *(fried dumplings)*

Pakoras are a type of fried dumpling or fritter, made using gram (chickpea) flour, and are a popular snack. You can turn these into onion bhajis by leaving out the potatoes and tomatoes.

## Makes about 20

## Ingredients

- 1 onion
- 3 spring onions
- 1 medium potato, peeled
- ½ tsp chilli powder
- ½ tsp turmeric powder
- 6 heaped tbsp gram flour
- 100g tinned chopped tomatoes
- 1 tbsp chopped fresh coriander
- Oil, for frying
- Plain yoghurt or chutney, to serve

## Equipment

- Mixing bowl
- Frying pan
- Deep, heavy-bottomed saucepan

**SAFETY FIRST**
Ask an adult for help when using a knife or a hob.

# Method

1. Cut the onion into quarters and then thinly slice.

2. Slice the spring onions into small pieces.

3. Cut the potatoes into chips, then slice each chip into the same size pieces as the spring onions.

4. Place everything in a bowl with the spices, gram flour and tomatoes, then mix well.

5. Add 2 tablespoons of water and stir to combine. You want a thick mixture that falls gently off a spoon. If the mixture is too thick, add another tablespoon of water. If the mixture is too runny, just add another tablespoon of gram flour to thicken.

6. Ask an adult to help you with the next bit. Heat about 5cm oil in a deep, heavy-bottomed saucepan to deep-fry the pakora.

7. When hot, gently drop teaspoons of the mixture into the pan. You will need to cook the pakora in small batches.

8. Fry for 5 minutes, then turn with a spatula and cook for a few more minutes. The pakoras are ready when the outsides are a deep golden-brown colour all over. Drain on kitchen paper and continue to cook until all the batter is used.

## TOP TIP:

You can add different chopped or small vegetables to the pakora batter, if you like. Try:

- Sweet peppers
- Spinach
- Sweetcorn
- Chillies

# Stuffed Dates

Dates are tasty on their own, but if you want to do something a bit different, you can stuff them for a delicious, special treat.

## Makes 12

## Ingredients

- 12 medjool dates
- 12 tsp crunchy peanut butter
- 1 tbsp desiccated coconut

**SAFETY FIRST**

Remember to ask an adult for help when using a knife, as they can be very sharp.

# Method

1. If your dates have stones, carefully slice halfway along one side and remove them. If not, you still need to make a cut along one side of each date – take care not to cut it completely in half.

2. Take 1 teaspoon of peanut butter and place it in the middle of the date. Push it down gently so it fills the gap completely.

3. Repeat with all the dates.

4. Sprinkle a little desiccated coconut over each date and they're ready to eat!

## TOP TIPS:

The stuffed dates look really pretty presented in colourful cupcake cases – the perfect gift!

You can use any kind of nut butter you like – smooth peanut butter, cashew butter, almond butter, it's your choice!

Instead of desiccated coconut, melt a little chocolate and drizzle it back and forth over the peanut butter-stuffed dates for an impressive-looking topping.

# Star-spangled Puffed Rice Treats

Transform ordinary puffed rice into something Eid-worthy with the addition of star-shaped sprinkles and melted chocolate.

## Makes 12

## Ingredients

- 100g milk chocolate
- 60g unsalted butter
- 90g puffed rice
- Multi-coloured star sprinkles

## Equipment

- Microwave-proof bowl
- 12 cupcake cases

# Method

1. Break the chocolate into small pieces and put in a microwave-proof bowl.

2. Melt the chocolate in the microwave in 10–20 second bursts, checking each time.

3. Cut the butter into small pieces and stir it into the hot melted chocolate until melted and well combined.

4. Add the puffed rice and stir until coated in the chocolate mixture, top with the star sprinkles.

5. Spoon the mixture into 12 cupcake cases and leave to cool and set.

# Baklawa (sweet pastries)

Baklawa is found in many cultures and is traditionally associated with the Middle East. There are many variations and you can adjust this sweet pastry recipe to use different nuts – pistachios, almonds and pecans – and flavours.

## Makes about 36

## Ingredients

### For the syrup

- 150g golden caster sugar
- 1 tbsp honey
- ¼ tsp ground cinnamon

### For the nut mixture

- 150g walnuts
- 25g pecans
- 1 tbsp honey

### For the pastry

- 150g butter
- 8 sheets of filo pastry, about 200g

## Equipment

- 2 saucepans
- Deep-sided baking tin

# Method

**1.** First, put all the ingredients for the syrup into a pan with 200ml water over a low heat. Stir occasionally, and when the sugar dissolves, turn the heat up slightly for 2–3 minutes, then take the pan off the heat and put to one side. Be very careful with hot syrup.

**2.** Preheat the oven to 200°C/400°F/Gas 6.

**3.** Melt the butter in a separate pan.

**4.** Put all the nuts in a food processor and blitz until finely chopped. Then put the nuts in a bowl with 3 tablespoons of the melted butter and the honey and mix.

**5.** Cut the filo pastry sheets in half – they should be the same size as the tin.

**6.** Brush the base and sides of the baking tin with melted butter. Place the first sheet of pastry in the tin to cover the base and brush the top with butter. Top with the next sheet and brush with butter. Repeat using 5 sheets in total.

**7.** Spread half of the chopped nuts on the pastry, then top with another sheet of pastry, and brush with melted butter. Again, repeat using 5 sheets in total, then spoon the rest of the chopped nuts on top.

**8.** Top with another 5 sheets of pastry, brushing each layer with melted butter. (You may have some pastry left over, but that's okay.) Brush the rest of the melted butter over the top.

**9.** Now you need to cut the pastry – ask an adult to help you with this bit. Cut the baklava into any shape you want (small rectangles are easier than diamond shapes). Make sure you cut all the way to the bottom.

**10.** Put the tin in the oven. After 15 minutes, turn the temperature down to 160°C/315°F/Gas 2¬–3 and bake for another 30 minutes.

**11.** Carefully take the tin out of the oven (ask an adult to help) and immediately pour over half of the syrup mix, making sure it gets into the gaps between the baklava pieces. Wait 15 minutes, then pour the rest of the syrup over.

**12.** Leave the baklava to cool completely – this will take a few hours. Then it's ready to eat!

# Halwa *(semolina pudding)*

There are different types of halwa, including a version made from vegetables such as carrots (most common in India and Pakistan), a version that is made using cornflour and sugar (most common in Somalia), and a version that uses semolina (found in India and even in Eastern Europe). This recipe makes the latter, and you can make it your own by including your favourite dried fruit and nuts.

## Serves 6

## Ingredients

- 150g sugar
- 2 tbsp ground cardamom
- 150g ghee
- 200g fine semolina
- 50g ground almonds
- Dried fruit and nuts (optional)
- Ice cream, to serve (optional)

## Equipment

- 2 saucepans

# Method

1. Put the sugar, cardamom and 600ml water in a saucepan and slowly bring to the boil. Turn down the heat and simmer for 2 minutes, until syrupy, before switching off and setting the pan one side.

2. Put the ghee in another pan and melt slowly. When melted, turn the heat to low and add the semolina. Cook the semolina for about 8 minutes, stirring, until nicely golden brown.

3. Add the ground almonds to the semolina mixture and mix together for 1 minute until combined.

4. Now, ask an adult to help with this bit. Pour a little of the sugar syrup mixture into the semolina pan. Take care as when the two mixes come into contact, they will bubble – you'll need to stir the mixture well.

5. Keep stirring the mixture as the adult adds the rest of the sugar syrup, a little at a time.

6. The mixture will start to thicken, but keep stirring (ask an adult to take over if your arms become too tired!) until the mixture starts to come away from the sides of the pan. It should be like a thick porridge.

7. If you're using dried fruit or nuts, stir them in now. Halwa is best eaten warm, and you can add a dollop of ice cream to the side if you like!

**SAFETY FIRST**
Ask an adult for help when using a knife or a hob.

# *Kheer* *(rice pudding)*

Kheer is a traditional Pakistani dessert that resembles rice pudding. The key to making this dish is to take it slowly, and have lots and lots of patience.

## Serves 4

## Ingredients

- 50g broken basmati rice
- Pinch of salt
- 500ml milk
- 5 tbsp sugar
- 4 crushed green cardamom pods

## Equipment

- Heavy-bottomed saucepan

**SAFETY FIRST**
Ask an adult for help when using a knife or a hob.

## Method

**1.** Rinse the rice three times and then put it in a saucepan with 300ml water on a low heat. Simmer very gently until the water is absorbed and the rice is very soft.

**2.** Add the salt and stir.

**3.** Add the milk to the rice and bring it slowly to the boil, stirring regularly.

**4.** Turn the heat to low and let the milk and rice simmer gently for 10 minutes, stirring every few minutes.

**5.** Add in the sugar and cardamom and stir in well. Continue simmering gently for around 30-45 minutes, stirring regularly.

**6.** The kheer will become thicker the longer you cook it and will continue to thicken as it cools, so keep simmering until you reach a consistency you think is slightly looser than you would like to eat.

**7.** You can eat the kheer hot or let it cool and enjoy it cold.

### TOP TIP:
If you like, add a couple of handfuls of raisins or nuts (almonds or pistachios work well) to the kheer just before you turn the heat off.

# Chocolate Fudge

This is a very simple recipe for chocolate fudge and makes a great gift. You can make this fudge using the microwave or on a hob.

## Makes about 36

## Ingredients

- 200g dark chocolate
- 200g milk chocolate
- 397g can condensed milk
- 25g butter
- 100g icing sugar

**SAFETY FIRST**

Ask an adult for help when using a knife or a hob.

## Equipment

- Deep-sided tray or baking tin
- Greaseproof paper
- Microwave-proof bowl or non-stick saucepan

## Method

1. Line a deep-sided tray or a baking tin with greaseproof paper.

2. Break the dark and milk chocolate into squares. If you're making the fudge in the microwave, put the chocolate into a microwave-proof bowl; for the hob put it into a non-stick saucepan.

3. Add the condensed milk and butter into the bowl or pan.

4. For the microwave, melt the mixture in 20 second bursts, mixing in between every burst. For the hob, melt the ingredients over a low heat, stirring frequently.

5. When the mixture has melted and is smooth and silky, sieve in the icing sugar. Mix thoroughly until you can't see any flecks of icing sugar.

6. Pour the mixture into the lined tray or tin and decorate, if you want (see Top Tip, below).

7. Put in the fridge until set, about 1 hour, then cut into squares. Your fudge is ready to gift or eat!

## TOP TIP:

You can decorate your fudge with a number of different yummy edible things. Just add one of the following, pressing them into the fudge before chilling. Choose from:

- Edible glitter
- Hundreds and thousands
- Chopped nuts
- Chopped dried fruit (like cranberries)
- Smarties

# Seviyan *(Vermicelli pudding)*

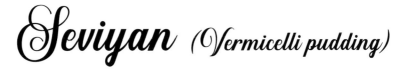

This traditional Pakistani dessert, also found in other South Asian cultures, is simple to make and great fun to eat – slurp up the noodles and then drink the sweet milk!

## Serves 4

## Ingredients

- 500ml milk
- 60g sugar
- 2 slightly crushed green cardamom pods
- 50g dried vermicelli noodles

## Equipment

- Saucepan

## Method

**1.** Put the milk in a saucepan and warm over a low heat. After 2 minutes, add the sugar and stir well.

**2.** Slowly bring the milk to the boil. (Milk can boil over quite easily so be extra careful and ask an adult for help!) When the milk starts to bubble slightly, add the cardamom pods.

**3.** Add the vermicelli and stir, keeping the milk boiling.

**4.** After 4 minutes, switch off the heat and set aside for 10 minutes. The dish may look quite liquid still, but the vermicelli will soak up the milk and thicken the pudding.

**5.** Remove the cardamom pods and eat hot or leave to cool and enjoy cold.

## TOP TIP:

This dish is lovely on its own, but for a special touch, top with one of the following:

- Sliced almonds
- Saffron
- Raisins
- Edible gold leaf

# Mango Lassi

Mangoes are juicy stone fruits that come in many different varieties. They're hugely popular because of their natural sweetness and can be used in lots of different recipes. Mango lassi is one of the most popular drinks, especially in Pakistan and India. Use fresh mango or, if they're not in season, mango pulp from a tin.

## Serves 4

## Ingredients

- 400g mango pulp
- 100ml milk
- 50g plain yoghurt
- 4 scoops vanilla ice cream

## Equipment

- Jug
- Whisk

# Method

**1**. Put the mango pulp, milk and yoghurt into a jug and whisk until smooth. (Or you can use a blender.)

**2**. Pour into four glasses, then add a scoop of vanilla ice cream to each glass.

**3**. Now, sit back and relax while you enjoy your refreshing treat!

# Lemon cooler

*Serves 4*

## Ingredients

- 3 lemons
- 3 tbsp granulated sugar
- 4 glasses of water
- Handful of fresh mint leaves

## Equipment

- Jug
- Whisk

## Method

**1.** Halve the lemons and squeeze the juice from them into a jug.

**2.** Add the sugar and water and whisk thoroughly until the sugar dissolves.

**3.** Pour into four glasses and add a couple of mint leaves to each glass.

**TOP TIP:**
You can make this lemon cooler more tart by using an extra lemon, or sweeter by adding a bit more sugar.

# Candyfloss cocktail

## Serves 4

## Ingredients

- Raspberry lemonade
- Pink candyfloss

## Equipment

- Cocktail sticks

**TOP TIP:**
You can use any fizzy drink you like, and even change the colour of the candyfloss from traditional pink to other colours.

## Method

1. Pour the raspberry lemonade into four glasses, leaving the a 4–5cm gap at the top of each glass.

2. With dry hands, carefully thread a cocktail stick through a piece of candyfloss.

3. Just before serving, balance a candyfloss stick on the top of each glass. Don't let it fall in, otherwise it will dissolve before anyone gets to see it!

# Watermelon Lemonade

## Serves 6

## Ingredients

- 2 small watermelons
- 1 litre lemonade
- ½ lemon
- Handful of fresh mint leaves

## Equipment

- Jug
- Whisk

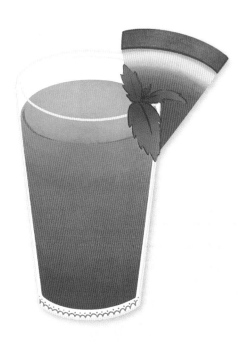

# Method

**1.** Halve both the watermelons. Put one half aside, and scoop the flesh out of the remaining three halves.

**2.** Mash the watermelon flesh through a sieve to remove all the seeds.

**3.** Put the mashed watermelon into a jug with the lemonade and mix together well with a whisk.

**4.** Pour the drink into six glasses.

**5.** Cut the lemon into 6 thin slices and place one in each glass, pushing them down into the drink to flavour it.

**6.** Ask a grown up to help you cut 6 small triangle wedges of watermelon from the reserved half in step 1.

**7.** Make a small cut down the middle of each wedge of watermelon and slide it on to the edge of each glass.

**8.** Add a few mint leaves to the top of the drink and enjoy!

# Falooda

Falooda is both a drink and a dessert! You'll need to start making it a few hours before serving, as the milk needs time to cool down.

## Serves 2

## Ingredients

- 2 tsp edible basil seeds
- 600ml milk
- 2 tbsp sugar
- 2 cardamom pods
- 50g falooda sev or dried vermicelli noodles
- 2 tbsp rose syrup
- 2 scoops vanilla ice cream

## Equipment

- Small saucepan

**SAFETY FIRST**
Ask an adult for help when using a hob.

# Method

1. Put the basil seeds on a plate and cover with water. Set to one side.

2. Put the milk and sugar in a small saucepan. Open the cardamom pods slightly, and add to the pan.

3. Bring the milk to the boil, then turn the heat down to low and simmer gently for 10–15 minutes.

4. Remove from the heat and leave the milk to cool for a few minutes, then sieve into a jug. Once the milk is cool enough to go in the fridge, chill for 3-4 hours.

5. Cut the falooda sev or vermicelli into 5cm long pieces.

6. Put a pan of water on to boil, then add the falooda sev or vermicelli and cook until soft, then drain. Leave to cool.

7. Assemble the falooda when everything is cool. Put 1 tablespoon of the soaked basil seeds – which should have expanded – into each of two glasses.

8. Divide the cooked falooda sev or vermicelli between the glasses.

9. Put 1 tablespoon of the rose syrup in each glass and top with the cooled milk. Stir well so that that rose syrup turns the milk pink.

10. Add a scoop of ice cream to each glass, and it's now ready to serve!

# My Eid-ul-Fitr

Date _____

I spent Eid with _____

I ate _____

My favourite part of the day was

_____

_____

_____

_____

# Draw a picture of your Eid-ul-Fitr outfit below!

# My Eid-ul-Adha

Date _____

I spent Eid with _____

I ate _____

My favourite part of the day was

_____

_____

_____

_____

# Draw a picture of your Eid-ul-Adha outfit below!

# My Plans and Goals

Eid is not just about celebrating and having fun at the end of Ramadan and Hajj. Both Eid-ul-Fitr and Eid-ul-Adha are also about helping others and improving yourself.

On this page, record three things you want to do in the next year to help other people. This might be saving some of your pocket money regularly to give to charity, or writing to a relative you haven't seen in a while. Or perhaps you're going to pick up rubbish to make the area you live in cleaner, or help your parents by doing some extra chores.

Whatever it is, write your goals down here and look at them regularly to make sure you're keeping up with them.

**1.** _____

_____

_____

_____

_____

**2.** _____

_____

_____

_____

_____

**3.** _____

_____

_____

_____

_____

# My Eid Memories

Use this space to keep a record of any special Eid memories.

_____

_____

_____

_____

_____

_____

_____

_____

# Glossary

**ALLAH:** the Arabic word for "God".

**ASR:** the late afternoon prayer in Islam observed by Muslims daily.

**CALLIGRAPHY:** a form of decorative handwriting or handwritten lettering.

**DENOMINATIONS:** a category or group.

**DUHUR:** the early afternoon prayer in Islam observed by Muslims daily.

**EID MUBARAK:** translated to "Blessed Festival" and is a greeting exchanged by Muslims on Eid day.

**EID-UL-ADHA:** this translates to the "Festival of the Sacrifice" and is the festival celebrated after Hajj.

**EID-UL-FITR:** translates to "Festival of the Breaking of the Fast" and takes place the day after the last fast of Ramadan.

**FIVE PILLARS OF ISLAM:** the five bases of the Islamic faith that each Muslim must observe. see also: **SHAHADA, SALAAH, ZAKAT, SAUM** and **HAJJ**.

**FAJR:** the dawn prayer in Islam observed by Muslims daily.

**FITRANA:** a charitable donation of food or roughly £5 made by Muslims who have completed Ramadan.

**HAJJ:** this is the Muslim pilgrimage to Mecca, which takes place in the last month of the Islamic year and which all Muslims are expected to make at least once during their lifetime if they can afford – and are physically and mentally able – to do so. It is one of the Five Pillars of Islam.

**IFTAR:** the meal eaten by Muslims after sunset during Ramadan when they have completed their fast for the day.

**IHRAM:** the white garments worn by pilgrims on Hajj. It can also refer specifically to the dress worn by male Muslims on their pilgrimage to Mecca, consisting of two white cotton cloths, one worn round the waist, the other over the left shoulder.

**IMAM:** the person who leads prayers in a mosque.

**ISHAA:** the nighttime prayer in Islam observed by Muslims daily.

**KABAH:** a building at the centre of Islam's most important mosque, the Masjid al-Haram in Mecca, Saudi Arabia. It is the most sacred site in Islam.

**KEBAYA KURUNG:** an Indonesian traditional blouse-dress.

**KHAMIIS:** also known as "thawb" or "thobe", this is an ankle-length, long-sleeved, gownlike garment worn by Muslim men.

**LAYLAT—AL—QADR:** this translates to "Night of Power" and refers to a special day that falls within the last ten nights of Ramadan.

**LUNAR CALENDAR:** a calendar based on the monthly cycles of the Moon's phases.

**MEDINA:** one of the three holiest cities in Islam, located in Saudi Arabia.

**MAGHRIB:** the sunset prayer in Islam observed by Muslims daily.

**MECCA:** considered the holiest city in Islam, located in Saudi Arabia.

**MINA:** one of the holiest sites in Islam, located in Saudi Arabia.

**MOSQUE:** place of worship for Muslims.

**PEACE BE UPON HIM (PBUH):** a phrase Muslims say whenever they say the name of any holy prophet or messenger, as a form of respect.

**PILGRIM:** a person who journeys to a sacred place for religious reasons.

**PROPHET:** a person who speaks for Allah, also called a messenger.

**QURAN:** the Islamic sacred book, believed to be the word of Allah.

**RAMADAN:** the ninth month of the Muslim year, during which strict fasting is observed from sunrise to sunset.

**SAFA AND MARWA:** two small enclosed mountains situated near the Kabah within the precinct of Masjid al-Haram.

**SALAAH:** prayer, which is an obligatory part of being a Muslim and one of the Five Pillars of Islam.

**SAUM:** fasting, which is an obligatory part of being a Muslim and one of the Five Pillars of Islam.

**SECT:** a group of people with somewhat different religious beliefs but who all branch from one large religion/belief.

**SHAHADA:** intention or proclamation of faith, which is an obligatory part of being a Muslim and one of the Five Pillars of Islam.

**SUHOOR:** a meal eaten before sunrise during Ramadan; the last meal before fasting begins for the day.

**TARAWEEH:** special night prayers observed during the month of Ramadan.

**ZAKAT:** charity, which is an obligatory part of being a Muslim and one of the Five Pillars of Islam.

# About the Author

**SARAH SHAFFI** is a writer, editor and journalist who loves nothing more than reading books and eating delicious food (favourites include her mum's chaat and her dad's biryani). She is passionate about making sure everyone sees themselves in books, and that we can all tell our own stories.

# About the Illustrator

**AALIYA JALEEL** is an illustrator who loves bright, pastel colour palettes and floral themes. Alongside being a freelance illustrator, she is a student at the University of Texas-Dallas, majoring in Arts & Technology with a concentration in Animation.